C000133696

SOUTHERN STEAM LOCOMOTIVE SURVEY

in the Southern Steam series

Southern Steam Locomotive Survey: Maunsell Early Classes
Southern Steam Locomotive Survey: Maunsell Later Classes
Southern Steam Locomotive Survey: Bulleid Merchant Navy Pacifics
Southern Steam Locomotive Survey: Bulleid West Country Pacifics
Southern Steam Locomotive Survey: Urie Classes
Southern Steam Locomotive Survey: Drummond Classes
Southern Steam Locomotive Survey: Adams Classes
Southern Steam in Action: 1
Southern Steam in Action: 2
Southern Steam in Action: 3
Southern Steam on Shed
More Southern Steam on Shed
Southern Steam from Lineside
Southern Steam—South and East
More Southern Steam—South and East
Southern Steam—South and West
More Southern Steam—South and West
Southern Steam on the Isle of Wight
Steam on the Brighton Line
Southern Steam in the West Country
More Southern Steam in the West Country
Southern Steam in Close-up
Southern Steam—Preserved
Southern Steam—Doubleheaded
Southern Steam Branch Lines
Southern Steam 1923–39

SOUTHERN STEAM LOCOMOTIVE SURVEY

BULLEID LIGHT PACIFICS

edited by Tony Fairclough & Alan Wills

 D. BRADFORD BARTON LTD

© Copyright D. Bradford Barton Ltd ISBN 085153 2721

Published by Enterprise Transport Books Ltd
3 Barnsway, Kings Langley, Hertfordshire WD4 9PW

Printed and bound in Great Britain by BPC Hazell Books Ltd

introduction

'She's in the shed!' The news that Pacific locomotive No. 21C102 *Salisbury* of the brand-new 'West Country' Class had arrived in the Wiltshire city a day before its official naming ceremony had spread like wildfire among the youthful railway fraternity, and on that Sunday morning of 8 July 1945, groups of boys in ones and twos could be seen converging on the locomotive depot. Up the entrance steps they crept, ducking under the timekeeper's window to avoid detection, then slipping quickly between the engines to see if the rumour was well-founded. Sure enough, there she was, standing in a patch of bright sunlight just inside No. 10 road. Quickly the eyes took in the general impression of the new Pacific and she was obviously a smaller cousin of the familiar 'Merchant Navy' 4-6-2s. Gradually the detailed differences were registered, the most obvious being the welcome reappearance of the bright malachite green livery which had disappeared from the other Southern locomotives beneath a coating of wartime black 'tar'. The wheels were black, as was the background of the nameplate *Salisbury* to which a shedman was adding the finishing touches. The coat-of-arms beneath the nameplate added a note of dignity, while the three yellow stripes running the length of engine and tender completed the cheerful finish. During the afternoon, Nos. 21C101/103 were seen heading westwards together, en route to Exeter and Plymouth respectively. On the following evening, a goodly crowd had assembled on Platform 5 at the station for the naming ceremony which was performed by the Mayor of Salisbury. After His Worship had driven the locomotive up to the signalbox and back, No. 21C102 remained in the bay so that the public could inspect the footplate. Now the lads with inside information had been told that the Pacific would work down to her new home at Exeter on the 8.20 p.m.

stopper, so there were a number ready with tickets to ride behind *Salisbury* as far as Dinton, some ten miles down the line. But after the stock had been marshalled in the station, the Pacific suddenly set off light at a rattling pace out of the platform and disappeared westwards and to everyone's disgust, one of Salisbury's run-of-the-mill 'T9s', No.310, backed down on to the train. Having paid good money for the tickets, the lads decided to make the journey, albeit with much muttering and grumbling. (Oh, what wouldn't we give now for just one run behind an old 'T9'!).

The production of 'West Countries' and the 'Battle of Britains' proceeded apace and before long they were to be seen on many of the express turns for long worked by the 'King Arthurs'. But it was on the lines west of Exeter that the engines made the biggest impact, for there the Maunsell Moguls had for many years held sway and the Pacifics represented a considerable increase in power. It was, for example, a great thrill to see the 'Atlantic Coast Express' hauled through to Padstow (where an enlarged turntable had been installed in 1947) by 'West Countries', usually No.21C107 *Wadebridge* and No.21C108 *Padstow* in the early days. Some later engines, from No.21C121 onwards, first ran in Kent and gave a boost to these important services down to the Coast. In all, 110 light Pacifics were built and if controversy surrounded the 'Merchant Navies', it was certainly true of the 'West Countries'. For while most railwaymen and observers would concede that the Southern needed a really powerful Class 8 express engine, much doubt has been cast upon the wisdom of building so many Class 7s. As express engines they would run like the wind, they steamed well and often it seemed that the harder they were hit the better they went. But one role they most certainly did not fulfil and that was as general purpose mixed-traffic engines, for although they performed magnificently in the 1948 inter-Regional trials against other mixed-traffics, they were never good common-user locomotives and rarely performed well in the hands of crews who were unfamiliar with their idiosyncrasies. Often both management and men cried out for something tough and rugged which could pull anything and go anywhere (say a Stanier Class 5 4-6-0!), and although the 'West Countries' had a surprisingly wide route availability they were not too happy on stopping passengers and freights because of their chronic addiction to slipping. The sixty engines which were modified during 1957–61 were certainly more reliable than in their original form but the increased weight imposed restrictions upon their use on lines previously open to the class.

However, in spite of many criticisms, the light Pacifics did provide the Southern with a fleet of powerful engines which were invaluable during those hectic periods of intense passenger traffic which were such a feature of that Region. The true worth of the 'West Countries' could, for example, be seen on busy Sunday evenings in the 1950s when thousands of National Servicemen were returning to their camps and then a good Pacific with a pair of experienced men on the footplate would make the running along the main line in real rollicking style. For the footplatemen the Pacifics posed numerous problems. The poor visibility, due primarily to the drifting exhaust, and the inaccurate steam reverser were perhaps the main worries to afflict drivers, while the narrow 8ft 6in enclosed cab could become extremely hot and with their voracious appetite for coal, the Pacifics made the task of the firemen very arduous. How truly did the unknown Hebrew prophet of old foretell the life of the Bulleid Pacific fireman when he wrote in the *Book of Genesis* 'By the sweat of thy brow shalt thou eat thy bread', for his life was hard. Yet there was also glory, for these engines were amongst the most famous performers of them all and examples were still hard at work until the final demise of Southern steam in 1967.

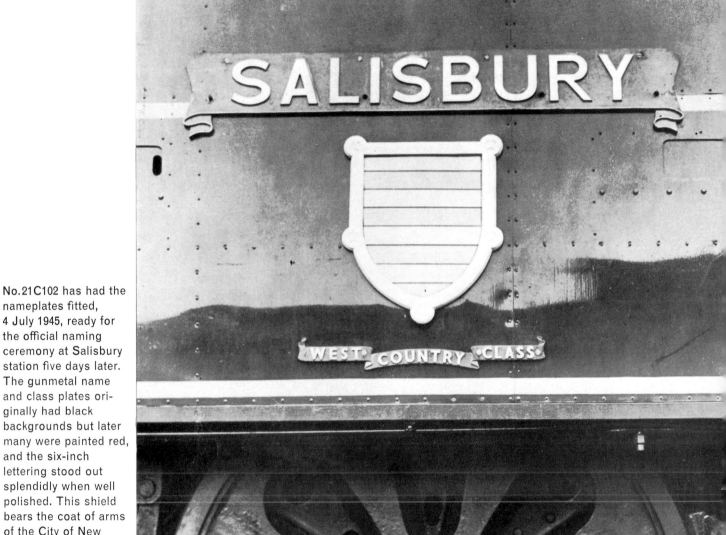

No.21C102 has had the nameplates fitted, 4 July 1945, ready for the official naming ceremony at Salisbury station five days later. The gunmetal name and class plates originally had black backgrounds but later many were painted red, and the six-inch lettering stood out splendidly when well polished. This shield bears the coat of arms of the City of New Sarum (Salisbury); similar shields were carried on some 'West Countries' while others carried the arms of their respective counties. Some, however, were without shields.

[Peter Winding Collection]

A 'West Country' Pacific in its natural environment: No. 21C116 *Bodmin* crosses the River Exe at Cowley Bridge Junction, outside Exeter, with a down Plymouth express on 26 August 1946. The first twenty engines of the class, each appropriately bearing the names of towns in the West of England, were allocated new to Exmouth Junction shed for working services out of Exeter.
[Brian A. Butt]

9

All but six of the 110 Bulleid light Pacifics were erected in the old-established Brighton Works of the Southern. The design work on the class was carried out in the Drawing office at Brighton, but much of the material was manufactured at Eastleigh. No.21C107 *Wadebridge* nears completion in the erecting shop in 1945, alongside older engines of LBSCR vintage. [Peter Winding collection]

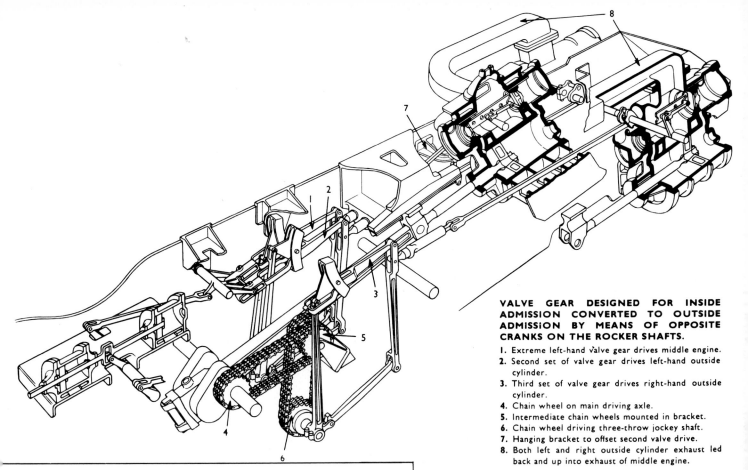

VALVE GEAR DESIGNED FOR INSIDE
ADMISSION CONVERTED TO OUTSIDE
ADMISSION BY MEANS OF OPPOSITE
CRANKS ON THE ROCKER SHAFTS.

1. Extreme left-hand valve gear drives middle engine.
2. Second set of valve gear drives left-hand outside cylinder.
3. Third set of valve gear drives right-hand outside cylinder.
4. Chain wheel on main driving axle.
5. Intermediate chain wheels mounted in bracket.
6. Chain wheel driving three-throw jockey shaft.
7. Hanging bracket to offset second valve drive.
8. Both left and right outside cylinder exhaust led back and up into exhaust of middle engine.

A diagrammatic view of the patent Bulleid variation of the Walschaerts valve gear as fitted to the 'West Country' class Pacifics. The CME was determined to avoid the overheating of the inside big-ends which so often beset the Gresley Pacifics with which he had worked for so many years, and the whole gear plus big-end and inside connecting rod were flood-lubricated in an oil bath. The thought of all this machinery thrashing about in 40 gallons of high-grade lubricating oil is awe-inspiring!

No. 21C107 *Wadebridge* as completed and posed for an official photograph. In Southern days the light Pacifics had black wheels and a black band painted below the bottom yellow stripe.
[L. T. George collection]

The 'West Countries' had few teething troubles and soon took over many of the passenger duties in the West of England. Often the engines were in service for some months before they were named, many having their nameplates unveiled at or near the station of the same name. No.21C142, seen hurrying westwards near Templecombe with a Plymouth express on 26 April 1947, was completed in the October of the previous year, but was not named *Dorchester* until 29 September 1948. [L. T. George collection]

No.21C113 (later *Okehampton*) hauls its complement of GWR coaching stock along the Western main line at Dawlish on 26 June 1946. Southern men from Plymouth (Friary) and Exeter (Exmouth Junction) sheds worked with their own engines, over the South Devon line in order to be familiar with the road in case of emergencies. The GWR men had reciprocal workings via Okehampton.   [L. T. George collection]

The light Pacifics began to work on Eastern Section services in 1946, and in the hands of Ramsgate men soon made their presence felt on the difficult routes down to the coast. A second batch, Nos. 21C133-40, went to Stewarts Lane, and the experts there took readily to the new motive power. Immaculate No. 21C135 (later *Shaftesbury*) was working an up boat train, near Shorncliffe in May 1947. [D. T. Cobbe]

14

The same engine was rostered to the 'Golden Arrow' one day in July 1946. The streamlined Bulleids always looked their best in the bright malachite green livery which, with the simple yellow lining, enlivened the austere outline of the boiler casing. [D. T. Cobbe]

Brand-new Pacific No.21C164, the 1000th locomotive to be completed at Brighton Works, stands with restored 'Terrier' No.82 *Boxhill* before a ceremony on 9 June 1947, in which the Mayor of Brighton declared the new engine 'ready for traffic'. In fact, the Bulleid was painted grey, with white lettering and was awaiting its 'top coat' of malachite green.

[Peter Winding]

No. 34057.   [D. M. Cox]

16

Nos. 21C149-70 and 34071-90/109-110 were identical with their sister engines but carried names associated with the Battle of Britain. No. S21C157 *Biggin Hill*, seen at Cheriton Junction with the 2.40 p.m. Folkestone Harbour to Victoria on 2 December 1948, is still in Southern malachite green livery, but has been lettered 'British Railways' and the handsome plaque has been removed from the smokebox. [D. T. Cobbe]

No. 34032 (later *Camelford*) takes it easily around the curves at Hawksbury Junction, Dover, with the 3.35 p.m. Margate–Charing Cross fast on 2 October 1948. Renumbered and lettered 'British Railways' the engine still retains its Southern smokebox plaque. [D. T. Cobbe]

A light-weight load for No. 34049 *Anti-Aircraft Command* on 9 April 1956. The 'Battle of Britain' is on one of Salisbury's London rosters which involved working home on a 'stopper' from Waterloo. These trains usually ran non-stop to Woking on the 'down through' (the scene here is at Surbiton), then calling at all stations to Salisbury.   [A. R. Butcher]

The nameplate and regimental crest of No. 34049.   [D. M. Cox]

Another Salisbury Pacific, this time the famous No. 34051 *Winston Churchill*, has a quiet siesta outside the old shed at Nine Elms, after taking on coal and water following its run up to Town. This was a favourable out-of-the-way spot where visiting engines could wait before returning to their home stations. No doubt the Salisbury men are enjoying a quick yarn with their Cockney colleagues in 'The Cabin', the enginemen's rest room, before they have to set to work on the second leg of their day's duty. [A. R. Butcher]

The world-famous nameplate and plaque. [A. R. Butcher]

With an axle-loading of 18¾ tons, the light Pacifics had a wide-ranging route availability and their first sphere of activity was on the lines west of Exeter, where their tractive effort of 31,000lb proved most welcome. No.34059 *Sir Archibald Sinclair* coasts downgrade towards Bere Ferrers with a Plymouth-bound express on 16 April 1954.   [Brian A. Butt]

The 'West Countries' were regarded as mixed-traffic engines and were often to be seen on freight turns; No. 34021 *Dartmoor* has been halted by signals alongside Plymouth (Friary) Locomotive shed on 29 August 1957. [A. R. Butcher] Below, No. 34035 *Honiton* calls at Sidmouth Junction with an Exmouth Junction–Yeovil pick-up goods, September 1959.

Dainton summit, that famous Western location, sees No. 34016 *Bodmin* at the head of the Exeter–Plymouth local on 26 August 1957. Of course, these lightly-loaded turns did not extend the Pacifics unduly, so there was little opportunity to compare performance with the 'native' Great Western 4-6-0s on this famous testing ground.   [A. R. Butcher]

The Bulleid light-weights replaced the Exmouth Junction 'Woolworths' (the 'N' Class Moguls) on the interchange workings between Plymouth and Exeter. Malachite-green No. 34019 *Bideford* steams along near Totnes with its mixture of G W R stock forming the 4.32 p.m. Plymouth to Exeter local on 8 August 1949.

[D. T. Cobbe]

Biggin Hill comes to Aller Junction: the driver of No. 34057 has shut off steam at the approaches to busy Newton Abbot while working a Plymouth to Exeter turn in September 1959.   [Derek Cross]   23

A Bulleid Pacific with
Bulleid coaching stock
climbs westwards out
of Wilton in the
summer of 1963.
'Battle of Britain' No.
34054 *Lord Beaverbrook*
of Exmouth Junction
shed has no problems
with the ten bogies as
it hammers up the
1 in 144 gradient. The
Bulleid boiler was a
wonderful steam-
producer and provided
the Pacifics did not
start slipping they were
very happy on these
West of England
banks.
　　[G. A. Richardson]

A Southern express heads Plymouth-wards out of Exeter (St. David's) behind No. 34056 *Croydon*, 24 August 1957. At that period, Exmouth Junction shed had a fleet of some thirty light Pacifics, many of which were used on duties to Plymouth, Padstow and Ilfracombe, lines which previously had seen nothing larger than Maunsell 2-6-0s. The track layout at St. David's was such that this *down* Southern train is heading towards its destination on the *up* Western metals. [A. R. Butcher]

Bulleid Pacifics at Exeter's other main station, Central, on 14 August 1952. No. 34022 *Exmoor* has worked in from North Devon with the Ilfracombe portion of the up 'Atlantic Coast Express', and having removed one coach has been replaced by 'Merchant Navy' No. 35025 *Brocklebank Line* for the continuation of the run to Waterloo.

[D. T. Cobbe]

No. 34084 (later *253 Squadron*) heaves its load up the 1 in 30 incline out of Folkestone Harbour station on 8 May 1950. Great care in handling the regulator would be required with a light-footed Pacific on such a gradient, and the presence of an Inspector on the footplate suggests a trial trip. [D. T. Cobbe]

The same locomotive again in action on 2 October 1957 when it was employed on the up 'Man of Kent' which is seen nearing the end of its trip as it crosses Hungerford Bridge at the approach to Charing Cross station. [A. R. Butcher]

Facilities for heavy repairs were provided at Bricklayers Arms (73B) shed in East London. The coupling and connecting rods have been removed from No. 34092 *City of Wells*, 2 April 1955. This locomotive, reputedly the best of all the light Pacifics at Stewarts Lane shed, carried the name *Wells* from November 1949 to March 1950.

[Brian Morrison]

Dense, dirty fog enveloped London as the 4.56 p.m. from Cannon Street to Ramsgate groped its way out of Town on 4 December 1957. With the fireman building up his fire for the climb to Knockholt, the driver looked for, but missed, the St. Johns outer and intermediate home signals. The fireman then spotted the inner home at red but too late, for No. 34066 *Spitfire* rolled on, in spite of an emergency brake application and ploughed into a stationary electric train. The subsequent derailment brought down an overhead bridge and the tragic accident resulted in 90 deaths among the passengers. No. 34066, damaged but not destroyed, is seen awaiting repair in Eastleigh Works on 15 February 1958.

[L. W. Rowe]

Stewarts Lane shed, in Battersea, London, always prepared the engine for the 'Golden Arrow' with meticulous care. For several years during the 1950s the prestige train was hauled by 'Britannia' Pacifics, but during its final years of running the task reverted to the Bulleid 4-6-2s. No. 34086 *219 Squadron* has had a thorough clean and has been fitted with the decorative arrows and flags which enhanced the glamour of this duty. [D. T. Cobbe]

No. 34086 again, this time seen hard at work on the 2.50 p.m. Folkestone Harbour–Victoria boat train near Shorncliffe on 15 April 1961. [D. T. Cobbe]

No. 34084 *253 Squadron* trundles past Folkestone Junction with a load of coal empties on 1 July 1960. The Eastern Section Pacifics had fewer freight turns than their sisters at Exmouth Junction; possibly this locomotive is working out its required mileage before paying a visit to the shops for a general overhaul. [D. T. Cobbe]

Following the successful modification of 'Merchant Navy' 4-6-2 No.35018 in February 1956, it was decided to rebuild the light Pacifics in a similar manner, the first engine so treated being No.34005 *Barnstaple* which emerged from East-leigh Works in its new guise in June 1957. As with the Pacifics in their original streamlined condition, it was difficult to distinguish at a glance the light Pacifics from the larger 'Merchant Navies'. The best clue for the observer was the shape and position of the nameplates, which were mounted immediately above the running plates on the 'West Country' and 'Battle of Britain' classes. This study shows the Ramsgate engine No.34082 *615 Squadron* in steam at Eastleigh shed on 26 April 1960, following its visit to the Works for modification. [L. Elsey]

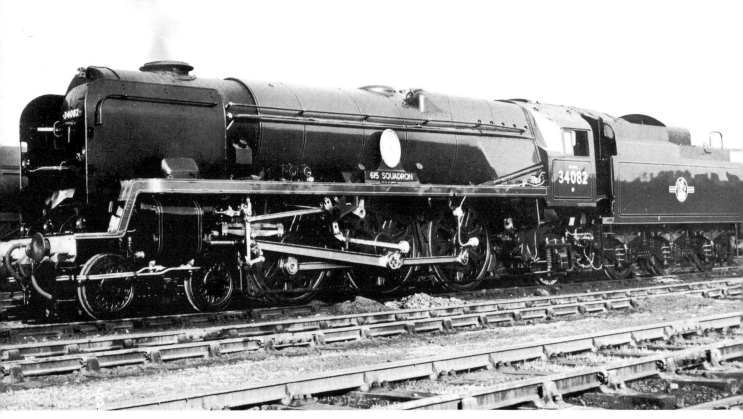

A close-up of the nameplate of No.34003 *Plymouth* which was modified in September 1957. The plates and shields were mounted on a metal framework, the shield being fitted above the nameplate on the rebuilt locomotives. In this view, the repositioned sandbox filler pipes can be seen close to the nameplate; the small wheel near the dome controls the main manifold which supplies steam to the footplate fittings.

[W. L. Underhay]

PLYMOUTH

WEST · COUNTRY · CLASS

When the modification of the Pacifics was finally decided upon, the removal of the Bulleid/Walschaerts valve gear was one of the first items to be considered. The Chief Technical Assistant (Locomotives) at Brighton, R. G. Jarvis, evolved an orthodox Walschaerts valve gear for each of the three cylinders, although the original outside cylinders with their outside admission piston-valves were retained, with a new steel casting providing the inside cylinder which had an off-set steam chest with an inside-admission valve in the conventional manner. The original engines had the piston rods and crossheads forged together; in the Rebuilds they were separated.   [T. P. Cooper]

The front-end of a 'West Country' Pacific. The Bulleid–Firth–Brown wheels helped to give these and other Bulleid designs their unique appearance, and it was claimed that these wheels, derived from American practice, were less liable to distortion, with the added advantage of a reduction in weight. The bogie design was largely based on the successful 'Lord Nelson' component.

[T. P. Cooper]

Open Day at Eastleigh Works on 11 April 1958, with newly-modified 'West Country' No. 34016 *Bodmin* on show to the visiting public. While lacking the mystique of the 'originals', the 'rebuilds' had a look of functional elegance about them which was not unattractive to the mid-century observer.

[A. R. Butcher]

No. 34016. This locomotive has been preserved by the Quainton Railway Preservation Society at Quainton Road station in Buckinghamshire.   [A. R. Butcher]

Several of the rebuilt Pacifics were at work on the Eastern Section by the late 1950s. Few teething troubles were experienced with these engines and the Management had no qualms about rostering a Rebuild to such an important duty as the Royal Train from Dover to Windsor on 28 March 1958. The superbly prepared No.34037 *Clovelly* is seen with its complement of Pullmans plus baggage van leaving Shorncliffe. On this duty the Southern used the British headcode for a Royal Train instead of its special route indications.

[D. T. Cobbe]

A useful, but less glamorous, duty for No. 34027 *Taw Valley*, also in 1958. The modified Pacific is seen passing Sandling with a loose-coupled freight, a duty for which the 'West Countries' were not entirely suited, as their low factor of adhesion hampered their braking ability, although the rebuilds were rather better than the originals in this respect, and were eventually upgraded to 6F in place of the original 5F classification.

[D. T. Cobbe]

Rebuilt 'Battle of Britain' No. 34060 *25 Squadron* sweeps majestically over Battledown flyover at Worting Junction, Basingstoke, with an up Bournemouth fast on 7 August 1965. The enclosed cabs became excessively hot during the summer months and the fireman is glad to have a breather before bending to his shovel once again.

[P. J. Lynch]

Just one month after emerging from Shops after rebuilding in May 1960, No. 34088 *213 Squadron* makes an impressive sight at the head of the 1.0 p.m. Victoria to Dover boat train. The engine has received full attention from the cleaner boys and has just coupled up to the train after dropping down to the terminus from Stewarts Lane shed. The oil lamp above the left buffer is the tail lamp for the tender-first trip from the shed, and the fireman can be seen removing the head code disc from the back of the tender. [C. E. Dann]

Driver Hickmott tightens the sandbox cover on No. 34088 while his mate removes the erstwhile tail lamp from the front of the engine. Southern Region top link men rarely had regular engines in the post war years, but some depots rostered picked engines to specific duties and these machines were usually well maintained, with the crews enjoying the luxury of first-class travel on their footplates! [C. E. Dann]

Following the electrification schemes in Kent during the early 1960s, the Pacifics were concentrated on the Western Section, where, with their larger 'Merchant Navy' cousins, they formed the mainstay of Southern express power until the final demise of steam in July 1967. Many of the migrating engines settled at Eastleigh shed, from which depot they worked the boat traffic from Southampton and certain of the Bournemouth turns. No.34025 *Whimple* pulls out of Waterloo for Bournemouth on a glorious spring morning in March 1964. [G. D. King]

No.34062 *17 Squadron* blackens the summer sky at Andover Junction as she restarts an up express from Exeter, in 1963. The Bulleid Pacifics were notorious for slipping, but fortunately the start from the up platform at this important station was downhill, a rare occurrence on the Waterloo–Exeter route.
[G. A. Richardson]

No. 34005 *Barnstaple* climbs away from Sidmouth Junction with a down express on 21 September 1963. The original 'West Countries' had steam sanders only on the middle and rear pairs of coupled wheels; the Rebuilds had this equipment on the first and second pairs, with the pipe arranged for reverse running on the rear coupled wheels. The driver is making full use of the sanders as he tackles the 1 in 300 gradient westwards

[W. L. Underhay

No.34037 *Clovelly* is
about to plunge into
the gloom of Honiton
Tunnel at the head of
the 11.45 Bude to
Waterloo summer
Saturday relief on 18
August 1962. The east–
ward climb to the tunnel
involved some 4½
miles at 1 in 90/100,
but it never seemed
quite so taxing as the
westward ascent with
the down trains.

[W. L. Underhay]

The rebuilt locomotives were heavier than in their original form and as such were prohibited from certain routes on which the unmodified light Pacifics were permitted. The one route west of Exeter which was open to the rebuilds was the Plymouth road, and Exmouth Junction's engines were to be seen heading many of the fasts from London along that line. No. 34109 *Sir Trafford Leigh-Mallory* drifts into Crediton with the 11.47 Exeter to Plymouth on 23 March 1963.

[W. L. Underhay]

Because of the restrictions imposed upon the rebuilt light Pacifics, the majority of Exmouth Junction's rebuilds were employed on the main line to Waterloo, where they performed with distinction. No. 34032 *Camelford*, at the head of an eastbound express, breasts the 1 in 100 summit at the mouth of Buckhorn Weston Tunnel, near Gillingham (Dorset) on 28 December 1962, just before the great blizzard swept the West Country.

[G. A. Richardson]

Bulleid activity at the Wiltshire station of Semley, 8 June 1964, as viewed by an enthusiastic photographer. Rebuilt 'West Country' No.34012 *Launceston* pulls away westwards with a three-coach Salisbury to Exeter local which will call at all stations on its 88-mile journey. [Derek Cross]

No. 34032 *Camelford* simmers quietly in the siding awaiting the passing of an up passenger before marshalling a milk train for London. The engine has little coal left on the tender, so she will probably only work to Salisbury.

[Derek Cross]

Once a favourite of Stewarts Lane shed, No. 34092 *City of Wells* hammers through Semley on the down road with a lengthy westbound freight. The crew will appreciate the empty stone hoppers next to the engine as these are vacuum braked and will provide additional braking power. The 'West Countries' were not popular motive power on loose-coupled freights because of their poor braking abilities. No. 34092 has been preserved at Haworth by the Keighley and Worth Valley Preservation Society.   [Derek Cross]

A Plymouth–Brighton through train hurries past Semley station behind No. 34084 *253 Squadron*. This was one of the few turns where engines were not changed at Exeter (Central), the light Pacific working through from Plymouth to Salisbury, where a Brighton locomotive took charge of the train for the remainder of the journey.

[Derek Cross]

'Battle of Britain' No. 34050 *Royal Observer Corps* also spent most of its working life at Salisbury, but this view shows the rebuilt Pacific on the turntable at Brighton shed. The plaque beneath the locomotive number is a representation of the Long Service Medal Ribbon. The ¾hp steam turbine which provides the power for the electric lights is visible beneath the cab.

[D. T. Cobbe]

Rebuilt No. 34052 *Lord Dowding* stands over the inspection pits outside Exmouth Junction shed on 11 July 1964. This depot, the first to receive Bulleid light Pacifics in 1945, maintained a large fleet of these engines until mid-1964. In 1957, for example, there were 28 on the depot's allocation, this number being retained until the big locomotive reshuffle at the close of the summer service in 1964. *Lord Dowding* was a long-standing Salisbury engine and has been turned ready for its run home later in the day.

[M. J. Messenger]

55

Following nationalisation, several 'West Countries' were to be seen on the Somerset & Dorset line, where they worked the 'Pines Express' and other heavy summer through trains from the Midlands and the North of England to Bournemouth. The Southern engines worked as far as Bath, over the fearsome gradients which abounded on that interesting route, but the S & D men were not too pleased with their Southern mounts and generally preferred the old favourites, the 'Black Fives'. The Bulleids' voracious appetite for coal and their propensity to slip did not endear them to enginemen who had to work lengthy trains over these steep grades. No. 34043 *Combe Martin* is seen in action with a twelve-coach load as she leaves Blandford Forum in June 1961.

[G. A. Richardson]

A 'Battle of Britain' in its proper shape! No.34070 *Manston* has steam up before departure from Exeter (Central) with the 1.10 p.m. stopping train to Salisbury on 9 September 1963. The coding above the number indicates that the locomotive was classified as 'Class 7 Passenger', 'Class 5 Freight', with the old Southern power group 'A' added. At that time, steam enginemen were being issued with French-style goggles, but they were not particularly popular with the old-timers.

[J. R. Besley]

On 20 February 1960, while working a Dover–Bricklayers Arms freight, 'Battle of Britain' No.34084 *253 Squadron* had the misfortune to be derailed near Hither Green. The locomotive rolled down an embankment, the crew fortunately escaping serious injury. It was not recovered until eight days later, and when seen at Eastleigh on 18 March, did indeed look a sorry sight. However, the chance may be taken of studying an 'unfrocked' Bulleid. In both views, the sandboxes are prominent underneath the boiler, while the two Ross pop safety valves show up well in the upper scene. The lower view gives some idea of the unusual shape of the fabricated smokebox, with the two feed-water pipes leading up to the clack boxes showing above the driving wheels which, of course, have no splashers fitted beneath the 'air-smoothed' casing.

[M. J. Jackson]   59

Possibly the easiest regular duty rostered to a British Pacific! During the winter timetable period, the 'West Country' which brought the down 'A.C.E.' into Padstow then ran back the 5½ miles to Wadebridge and coupled up to the single coach which formed the stock of the 6.13 p.m. unadvertised workmens' to Padstow. No. 34110 *66 Squadron* heads towards the terminus on 16 May 1962. Below, the final part of the Pacific's roster was to bring the coach back to Wadebridge at 6.40 p.m., then the engine went on to the shed to be 'squared up' for the night. No. 34033 *Chard* skirts the beautiful estuary of the River Camel on its way to Wadebridge on 17 May 1962. It was duties such as this which evoked the oft-heard criticism that the Pacifics were under-worked! [D. T. Cobbe]

The up 'A.C.E.' departed from Padstow at 9.33 a.m. during the summer service. Here, 'Battle of Britain' No. 34078 *222 Squadron* blows off at 250lb/sq.in as she collects the stock from the siding before shunting into the platform to collect the passengers. Originally the boiler pressure of all the Pacifics was 280lb/sq.in, but R. G. Jarvis decided on the lower pressure to ease both the general maintenance problems and also the difficulty of getting the injectors to work against the very high boiler pressure. Another problem for firemen was that the light Pacifics had no front dampers and it was difficult to control the combustion rate when standing.

[D. T. Cobbe]

The air-smoothed Pacifics were always plagued by the problem of drifting exhaust obscuring the forward vision. When built, short deflectors were fitted, but over the years these were extended, a few, as on No. 34006 *Bude,* being of extreme length. Others also had the deflectors curved as on No. 34095 *Brentor,* seen in the background on Branksome shed, 19 June 1960. [G. A. Richardson]

No. 34049 *Anti-Aircraft Command*, of Salisbury shed, seen on the turntable at Exmouth Junction on 17 April 1960, had the top cowling altered in order to improve the upward air-flow, with a pair of small deflectors fitted alongside the chimney. Unfortunately this and other experiments made no appreciable difference to the exhaust problems.

[D. T. Cobbe]

The 5.12 p.m. 'stopper' to Waterloo pulls away under the magnificent upper quadrant gantry at the east end of Basingstoke station, 19 July 1963. The engine, No. 34099 *Lynmouth*, is from the Salisbury shed, and has been given the cleaning treatment usually associated with that Wiltshire depot during the last ten years of steam.

[W. L. Underhay]

No. 34007 *Wadebridge* illustrates a principal Pacific problem—the fight for adhesion. With a tractive effort of 31,000lb and 18$\frac{3}{4}$ tons on each coupled axle, the 'West Countries' had a factor of adhesion of 4·06, which, combined with a tendency for the Pacific to 'sit back' on its pony truck when starting, provided the ingredients for the tremendous slipping which often afflicted these engines. Here, *Wadebridge*, slipping violently, is lifting a heavy Weymouth–Waterloo express around the curve at Poole, with the steam sanders working, safety valves blowing off, cylinder cocks open, the whistle gland leaking and over all, a towering column of smoke and steam belching from the chimney. As a point of interest, The Quainton Railway Preservation Society aim to preserve this locomotive.

[G. A. Richardson]

'West Countries' were often called upon to work enthusiasts' specials, sometimes on foreign metals. One famous occasion was the run of the 'Cornubian' to Penzance and back to Plymouth on 3 May 1964 to mark the farewell of steam power in Cornwall. The Plymouth Railway Circle and RCTS chose No. 34002 *Salisbury* for the nostalgic run, probably the only occasion that a 'West Country' reached the GW terminus at Penzance. The Southern Pacific is much admired as she stands against the background of the typical Great Western wooden buildings at Bodmin Road.

[D. H. Ballantyne]

Immaculate Exmouth Junction Pacific No.34079 *141 Squadron* at the head of a special in Bristol Temple Meads on 14 June 1964. When, towards the end of the steam era, engines were used on 'foreign' lines for enthusiasts' specials, local enginemen usually crewed the locomotives and, generally speaking, these men found the Bulleids difficult to handle. However, these Pacifics were not complete strangers at Bristol as Salisbury 'Spare Gang' men occasionally worked in with excursions from the south coast during summer weekends.

[D. H. Ballantyne]

Bournemouth Top Link men had two long-standing turns to Oxford, often taking 'West Countries' to this important rail centre. Back in 1957 (2 November) the old tradition of only sending your best engines into foreign territory was still strictly adhered to, and No. 34040 *Crewkerne* looks neat and tidy alongside the station pilot No. 6970 *Whaddon Hall* as she pulls away with a Birkenhead to Bournemouth express.

[P. Q. Treloar]

No. 34109 *Sir Trafford Leigh-Mallory* enters Oxford over the Canal Bridge with a van train on 26 October 1963. [D. M. Cox] Below, by 1961, the rot had set in, and the 'West Country' at the head of the 8.30 a.m. Newcastle–Poole on 2 September certainly does not look like one of Bournemouth's 'best' engines. No. 34034 *Honiton* is assuredly not a good advertisement for the Southern in this Western stronghold.

[W. L. Underhay]

How the men hated foggy conditions on the London road, especially when the run had to be made with an original Bulleid! This driver is adding to the general smog at Bournemouth (Central) by lighting his pipe before ascending the footplate of No. 34102 *Lapford*, one of Bournemouth's 'West Countries'. The worst turns of all were the late evening runs up to Waterloo, when the fog and gloom always seemed at its most dense.

[G. A. Richardson]

A complete contrast, just a few weeks earlier at Bournemouth, on 4 October 1962. The sun shines brightly and all's well with the world as No. 34064 *Fighter Command* of Eastleigh shed steams away from Bournemouth (Central) with an afternoon express to London. This Pacific was fitted with a Giesl oblong ejector in April 1962. Seven nozzles were situated beneath the narrow chimney through which the exhaust came with great velocity, lifting high above the cab. This was the most successful solution to the problem of forward vision and plans were afoot to convert the majority of the light Pacifics, but by 1963 the writing was on the wall for steam and the expenditure was not authorised.
[G. A. Richardson]

The Giesl-fitted No. 34064 *Fighter Command* sweeps through Clapham Junction with the 11.30 a.m. Waterloo–Bournemouth on 10 June 1964. For many years this turn formed part of an Eastleigh Top Link roster—up 7.22 a.m. Southampton–Waterloo, down with the 11.30 a.m. with the first crew relieved at Winchester, then on to Bournemouth, returning with the 5.30 p.m. to London, the men again getting relief at Winchester, the third set of men bringing the engine home to Eastleigh with the 10.30 p.m. Mail from Waterloo. Over the years, Eastleigh men had worked these turns with Drummond T9s, Urie N15s, Maunsell 'King Arthurs' and 'Lord Nelsons' and finally the Bulleid 'West Countries' and 'Battle of Britains'—of which *Fighter Command* was reputed to be one of the very best.

[P. J. Lynch]

Unrebuilt 'Battle of Britain' 4-6-2 No.34081 *92 Squadron* makes a spirited getaway from Templecombe with the 9.0 a.m. Waterloo to the West of England on a bleak and wintry day in March 1963. The plain stove-pipe chimney of the original design can be seen clearly on this locomotive which, fortunately, is the subject of a preservation project by the Battle of Britain Locomotive Preservation Society.   [G. A. Richardson]

SEATON

WEST COUNTRY CLASS

No.34020   [D. M. Cox]

No. 34020 *Seaton*, about to enter the gloomy mouth of Blackboy Tunnel, between St. James's Park, Exeter, and Exmouth Junction, with the 4.42 p.m. Exeter–Salisbury on 3 August 1963. Judging by the coal on the tender, it looks as if the Exmouth Junction coal hopper has been living up to its reputation of being a 'coal smasher'; the enginemen always claimed that the Nine Elms hopper was much kinder to the larger lumps of fuel. [W. L. Underhay]

Southern trains passed through Western territory at Exeter (St. David's) station. Here, No.34110 *66 Squadron* eases away from the down platform with its up train, the 8.55 a.m. Ilfracombe–Salisbury slow, 9 June 1962.

[W. L. Underhay]

A rebuilt Pacific standing on the same spot but viewed from a different angle; No. 34056 *Croydon* waits for the road before proceeding around to the left and up the 1 in 37 incline to Southern territory at Exeter (Central). Photographed on 23 July 1962, this is the Plymouth–Brighton through train. The left-hand lifting bracket, one of the two which were fitted only to the light Pacific tenders, can be seen near the rear of the water tank.

[J. R. Besley]

During the early 1960s, the loads of the expresses generally became a little lighter and light Pacifics could be seen on turns which before were the exclusive preserves of the larger and more powerful 'Merchant Navy' Class. No. 34056 *Croydon* makes a steamy exit from Exeter (Central) with the up 'A.C.E.' at 12.30 p.m. on 2 September 1963. In earlier years, the disc headboards were always kept whitened by the storemen in the locomotive depots and such filthy route indicators as these would never have been tolerated.

[J. R. Besley]

Rebuilt 'West Country' No. 34017 *Ilfracombe* powers the diverted 'Bournemouth Belle' through Alton on 24 April 1966. Although recorders have timed light Pacific performances which seemed indistinguishable from those of their larger 'Merchant Navy' cousins, the footplatemen knew the difference, as the smaller engines had to be worked much harder, which meant additional coal-heaving and, should the boiler pressure fall below 200lb/sq.in, then the 'West Countries' would begin to flag, whereas the larger machines would storm on regardless.

[D. T. Cobbe]

No.34082 *615 Squadron* undergoing a heavy general repair in Eastleigh Works on 11 April 1958. The thin sheet metal of the streamlined casing was often damaged and the newly riveted sections will be noted. The 'West Country' boiler was a smaller version of the famous 'Merchant Navy' steam raiser and was tapered on its underside, contrary to the usual British practice. Heated by a grate area of 38sq.ft, this Bulleid boiler proved a prodigious producer of steam.

[A. R. Butcher]

An unidentified rebuilt light Pacific in Eastleigh erecting shop on 6 March 1965. The original 16¾in by 24in outside cylinders were retained, the right-hand piston being visible following the removal of the cylinder head. Although a new smokebox of orthodox design was provided at modification, the original eliptical smokebox door was retained thus helping to retain the 'Bulleid flavour' of the engines.

[D. M. Cox]

No. 34090 was rebuilt in April 1960 and was on Eastleigh shed, in company with unrebuilt No. 34041 *Wilton*, on 1 May 1965. It will be noted that the latter engine was one of the Pacifics which did not have a shield to accompany the name.

[D. M. Cox]

One of the reasons Bulleid put forward for the streamlining of his Pacifics was that cleaning would be much easier. True, the flat sides were straightforward enough, but unfortunately a ladder was required, not only for cleaning, but also for reaching the sandbox fillers and the boiler components. This Nine Elms cleaner-boy is giving No. 34090's magnificent nameplate a final polish. This engine was chosen to commemorate the old Railway Company and was named *Sir Eustace Missenden —Southern Railway* and when photographed in February 1959 was still in its original form.

[C. E. Dann]

Cleaning the rebuilds was somewhat easier as a running plate was provided above the driving wheels. However, cleaner-boys of average height could not reach the dome and the top of the boiler and they often succumbed to the temptation and did not climb up on the handrail in order to complete the work—the result being a streak of grime along the top of the locomotive! These Bournemouth lads are at work on No. 34024 *Tamar Valley*.   [D. M. Cox]

September 1965, and the run-down of steam is very apparent in this lineside photograph of No. 34040 *Crewkerne* taken at Battledown Flyover, Worting Junction, as the filthy Pacific heads a down express to Bournemouth.   [D. M. Cox]

Perhaps the most historic Bulleid journey of them all—No. 34051 *Winston Churchill* appropriately hauls the great statesman on his last journey, from Waterloo to Handborough, on 31 January 1965. With Driver Hurley and Fireman Lester of Nine Elms on the footplate, the beautifully prepared engine hauls the funeral train past Barnes. Fortunately this famous locomotive has survived the scrapping holocaust and eventually will be restored to exhibition standards.

[D. Trevor Rowe]

By way of contrast, Nos. 34006 *Bude* and 34057 *Biggin Hill* have been given the full treatment in order to work a 'Last Day' farewell special over the Somerset & Dorset Line. This train, which ran on 5 March 1966, was one of the most-photographed specials during the final years of steam.

[M. J. Fox]

Rebuilds in close-up: Nos. 34087 *145 Squadron* and 34100 *Appledore* stand together at Eastleigh shortly before the end —21 May 1967. The rebuilds had two-section rocking grates and hopper ashpans to speed the work of disposal. The electric headlamps were much brighter than the traditional British oil-lamps, and on foggy nights many drivers slipped some paper behind the lens in order to reduce the glare!

[Philip D. Hawkins]

A Bulleid line-up at Salisbury on 26 June 1966; Nos. 34100 *Appledore*, 34002 *Salisbury* and 34032 *Camelford*. The battery box for operating the A W S can be seen mounted between the frames above the buffer beams of each engine.

[D. T. Cobbe]

Nos. 34056 *Croydon* and 34004 *Yeovil* at Salisbury in February 1967. Above the first pair of coupled wheels can be seen two mechanical lubricators, the front one being a Wakefield for lubricating the right-hand cylinder, the rear a Silvertown for the axleboxes. Two further Wakefields for the middle and left-hand cylinders are situated on the opposite running plate.

[N. E. Preedy]

Fifty of the light Pacifics remained unmodified, as it was decided in 1961 that the short expectation of life for steam did not justify the expense involved. Two 'originals' Nos. 34102 *Lapford* and 34023 *Blackmore Vale* remained in service until the end of steam in July 1967, and were much in demand for special working. No. 34023 is seen at Wareham on 7 May 1967. Over the years, the 'originals' saw a number of changes. The smoke deflectors were lengthened, the cab received a wedge-shaped front, the valances were removed from the front of the cylinders, and AWS as well as speedometers appeared in the early 1960s. The tenders were considerably altered, so that they were more convenient to work on, but less attractive without their high sided raves. But basically the locomotives remained much as Bulleid conceived them, though with the reduction of the boiler pressure from 280 to 250lb/sq.in, the theoretical tractive effort came down from 31,000lb to 27,000lb but little or no difference was noted in the performance on the road.

[A. R. Butcher]

The shaft of the screw reverser angles down from the cab of No. 34001 *Exeter*, to connect with the Walschaerts valve gear below the running plate. The steam reverser was one of the most suspect items of the original design, as it was very difficult to set accurately, and even then they were liable to creep towards the longer cut-off position, a situation which was brought to the notice of the fireman when his fire started to dance about the firebox and then disappear up the chimney. It is rumoured that some drivers set the lever at 25 per cent then shut off the steam supply to the reverser and drove on the regulator alone—quite against regulations of course. The young crew of the Pacific have posed for the cameraman at Eastleigh on 3 April 1964. One wonders whether they survived the massive redundancies and transferred to the new forms of traction?

[N. E. Preedy]

At night, a steam engine seems more alive than ever. The glare from the firebox reflecting against the steam, the glowing cinders falling into the ashpan, the rumble of boiling water and the hiss of steam—all this emphasised the appeal of the iron horse. No. 34037 *Clovelly* brings life to Brockenhurst station on a January evening in 1967. Although this was the last year of Southern steam working, the engine is in fine external condition. The light from the firebox outlines the rearward facing windows which gave the crew good protection when running tender-first. [D. M. Cox]

The final week of Southern steam operation sees No. 34060, minus its *25 Squadron* nameplates, standing in the sunlight and shadow of Nine Elms shed, on 4 July 1967. This great London depot had been the home of many famous engines, with light Pacifics forming a considerable percentage of its main line strength in the post-war years. In 1957 for example, there were fourteen, which were hard-worked on the Bournemouth and Exeter turns. Today, the shed is but a memory, with the new Covent Garden market on the site where once generations of railwaymen laboured. [D. M. Cox]

Nos.34056 *Croydon* and 34071 *601 Squadron* in repose inside Salisbury shed. Thanks to the enthusiastic management, combined with a good number of cleaners, this depot was able to maintain its engines in clean condition until the final cessation of steam working and *Croydon* has obviously had a good polish during its sojourn inside the building. In the background can be seen the notice board with the enginemens' link rosters displayed—No.1 'Main Line', No.2 'Mixed Traffic', No.3 'Spare Gang', No.4 'Jubilee Gang', No.5 'Heavy Goods' and so on, duties which had been worked since the turn of the century and which would be completely metamorphosised at the great divide in July 1967.

[D. M. Cox]

Rebuilt 'West Country' No.34018, formerly *Axminster*, rounds the curve at Redbridge, shortly after leaving Southampton Docks with a banana special for Westbury, 19 June 1967. The nameplates and shield have been removed, leaving the bare metal supports on the running plates.

[D. M. Cox]

Rebuilt 'West Country' No.34098 *Templecombe* drops back over Canute Road into the Old Docks at Southampton in order to pick up a London-bound boat train, 14 March 1963.

[G. P. Brown]

At 9.16 a.m. on Saturday 8 July 1967 the last steam-hauled commuter train into Waterloo, the 6.49 a.m. from Salisbury, eased up to the buffer stops with No.34052 *Lord Dowding* proudly at its head. If loads exceeded twelve bogies the drivers compressed the hydraulic buffers in order to clear the points at the other end of the platform.

[P. Q. Treloar]

The first withdrawals of Bulleid Pacifics came in June 1963 when four 'originals', Nos. 34035/43/55/74 were scrapped, the last mentioned having completed a mere fifteen years of service. The first modified locomotive to go, No. 34028, was taken out of service in May 1964, eighteen years to the month after being built at Brighton, and only six years after its £9,000 rebuild. Thirty-six light Pacifics saw service in 1967, of which two 'originals' and nineteen 'rebuilds' remained in action at the bitter end on 9 July. However, all is not lost for at the time of writing, eight of these machines, Nos. 34007/16/23/39/51/81/92/105, have been, or will be restored to their former glory. The first to raise steam again was No. 34023 *Blackmore Vale*, thanks to the efforts of the Bulleid Society. The scene is the Longmoor Military Railway, 8 June 1968.   [D. T. Cobbe]